An Album of Stereographs

DATE DUE

JUN 9 1977		
AUG. 3 0 1980		
NO 2 8 '08		
Dec 16		

779.9
Da   Darrah, William Culp, 1909-
          An album of stereographs or, "Our country
      victorious and now a happy home; "from the
      collections of William Culp Darrah and Richard
      Russack.   Garden City,N.Y., Doubleday, 1977.
          109p.   illus.

          1.Stereoscopic views. 2.Wit and humor,
      Pictorial. I.Russack,Richard,jt.auth. II.Title.
      III.Our country victorious and now a happy home.

For Betty Heller

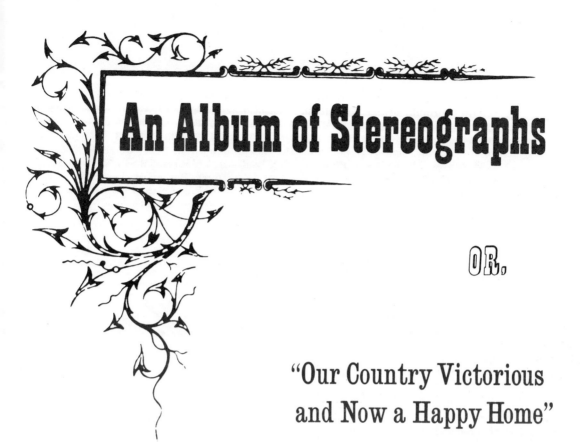

An Album of Stereographs

OR,

"Our Country Victorious
and Now a Happy Home"

*From the Collections
of William Culp Darrah
and Richard Russack*

Doubleday & Company, Inc.
Garden City, New York
1977

The stereographs on page 20, top, "Stolen Kisses Sweetest Are," copyright 1906 by Griffith & Griffith, George W. Griffith, Publisher; page 106, top, "A train robber holding up a train," copyright 1909 by H. C. White Co., H. C. White Co., Publisher; page 106, bottom, "A Case of Ale (Ail)," copyright 1908 by H. C. White Co., H. C. White Co., Publisher; and page 109, bottom, "The absent minded barber," copyright 1908 by C. H. Graves, The Universal Photo Art Co., Publisher, are reprinted with the permission of the Keystone View Company, 2212 East 12th Street, Davenport, Iowa. The stereograph on page 49, top, "The Automobile Somnambulist," copyright 1906 by Underwood & Underwood, is reprinted with the permission of Underwood & Underwood News Photos, Inc.

Library of Congress Cataloging in Publication Data
Main entry under title:

An Album of stereographs.

  1. Stereoscopic views. 2. Wit and humor, Pictorial.
I. Darrah, William Culp, 1909–   II. Russack,
Richard. III. Title: Our country victorious and now a
happy home.
TR780.A4   779′.9′97380207
ISBN: 0-385-11107-x
Library of Congress Catalog Card Number 76–23805

CONTENTS

A Special Mention

The editors would like to thank the two gentlemen who permitted us to select these slides from their extensive collections. William Culp Darrah has written about stereographs as well as collected them; he is the author of *Stereo Views: A History of Stereographs in America* and is completing *The World of Stereographs*. Richard Russack is president of the National Stereoscopic Association. Both were most generous with us. We would also like to thank Mrs. Rose Kramer for the loan of the series of eighteen cards which opens the "Connubial Bliss(ters)" chapter; our pleasure in them brought about this book.

A Note

t the turn of the century home movies were still a long way from being invented, and books and magazines were, for the most part, still being illustrated by woodcuts. Families in the East could not know what Yosemite really looked like and those in the West could not "really see" Niagara Falls or Saratoga. The solution was simple: nearly every home had a box of stereo views, or stereographs as they are more properly called. The stereograph first became popular in this country in the mid-1850s and that popularity continued into the 1930s.

Much of the history of the late nineteenth century was recorded by the stereo photographer: the Civil War, the building of the transcontinental railroad, Lincoln's funeral, the 1876 Centennial celebrations, the changing face of our cities, and, of course, the famous people of the day. This continued into the early twentieth century with views again of wars, presidents, industries, and humor. It is with this last group, the humorous subjects, that this volume is principally concerned.

Before 1870 stereographs were for sale by photographers, bookstores, novelty shops, at the corner drugstore and the general store, and by mail order across the country at prices ranging from fifteen cents to fifty cents each. There were literally thousands of photographers and publishers producing them commercially. In the

1870s inexpensive stereographs were produced to sell at five or ten cents each, and after 1880 door-to-door salesmen distributed them throughout the United States and Canada. By the early 1890s means had been developed to mass produce high quality stereo views at prices everyone could afford. Door-to-door selling methods were perfected, and the major publishers employed thousands of clean-cut young people to sell them in nearly every community. Mail order firms like Sears, Roebuck sold lithographed stereo views for eighty-five cents per hundred and the price for the stereoscope with one hundred cards was ninety-five cents.

The popularity of stereo views went through peaks and valleys over the years. They were first brought to the public's attention by Queen Victoria at the London Crystal Palace in 1851, although English photographers had been producing them earlier. Originally, viewing devices were cumbersome and not inexpensive. America's Oliver Wendell Holmes invented the stereoscope that most of us are familiar with: a device with a lens mounted at one end, usually with a hood, and a movable gadget to hold the view at the end opposite the lenses. The earliest views were daguerreotypes (on silvered copper). In 1852 the paper print from glass negatives replaced the daguerreotype because it permitted multiple copies. Two nearly identical images, often produced with cameras specially made for the purpose, were pasted on cardboard; when one looked through the viewer, one could see true-to-life three-dimensional images.

Eventually nearly every American family had a basket of views and a viewer—or had an aunt or a cousin who did. And over the decades countless evenings were whiled away with that basket of slides, and countless summer afternoons on the front porch, as the magical pictures took the beholder on a trip around the world or to the horrors of war at the Gettysburg battlefield. Almost every town had its stereo photographer who, in addition to his regular line of subjects, could be hired to take stereo views of family gatherings, new homes, and even dead relatives. Developers of a town in Illinois had pictures taken to help sell land, Greenwood Cemetery commissioned a large set of views to show the newest Victorian-style burial ground, merchants gave away stereo views of their stores and workrooms. Among the most popular topics, from the very outset, were the humorous and sentimental stereographs, single moments of comedy or series of two or more that told a story. The examples collected here were made in the closing years of the nineteenth century and the first decade of the twentieth.

Certain themes were particular favorites, and we have sometimes included more than one version of the same idea to illustrate the most popular situations. The humor dwelled most lingeringly on home and family life, and courtship, and scenes from boarding school and college. The demure young woman who turns into a termagant matron, the bearded farmer with his rustic ways, the incorrigible husband who stays out late drinking with his cronies, the strict parents overseeing Daughter's virtue, and Daughter's own pleasure in trapping and teaching a lesson to forward young men—all were staples of the comedy of the day. And there is also some cheesecake, some daring show of a bare leg, or for that matter a stockinged leg, here and there.

From this distance it looks like a pleasant world, if an encumbered one all around. The Spanish-American War had ended to everyone's satisfaction, and the years that followed, as illustrated by the slides in this book, put on a show of family solidarity and respectable living (if of course one doesn't count a touch of class snobbery and the casual patronage of the newly arrived immigrant). But as the stereographs also show, the solidity was often an illusion. What they found to laugh at in themselves often comes nearer vaudeville than wit. Still, there is genuine fun here and fresh delight all these years later.

A Mellow Drama

"I am so Sorry to Leave You, dear."

"My Country Calls, and I Must Go."

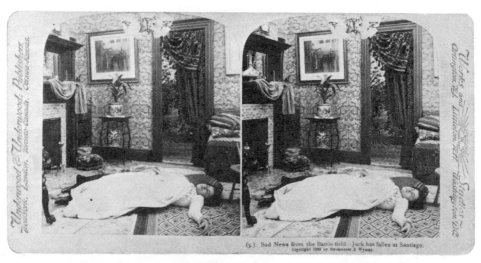

Sad News from the Battle-field—Jack has fallen at Santiago.

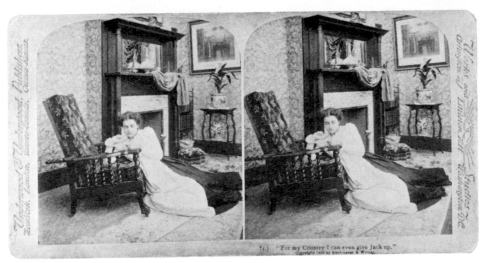

"For my Country I can even give Jack up."

"Oh Jack! Jack—Not Killed, but Only Wounded!"

The Story of the Battle—Our country victorious and now a Happy Home.

COURTSHIP
(Before the Fall)

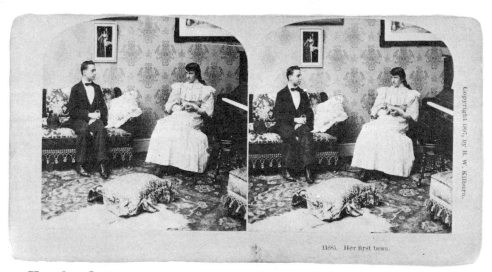

Her first beau.

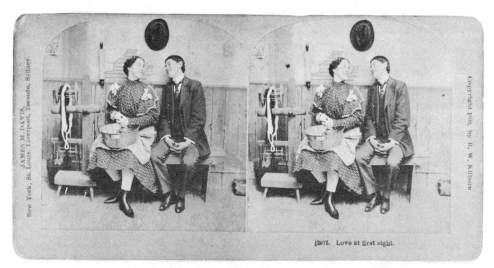

Love at first sight.

When the Frost is on the Pumpkin and the Fodder is in the Shock.

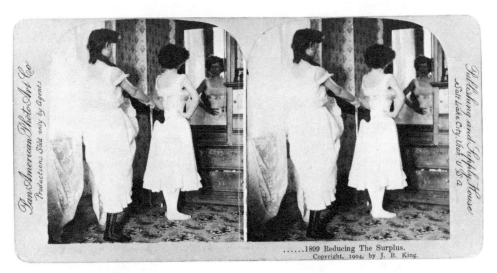

Reducing The Surplus.

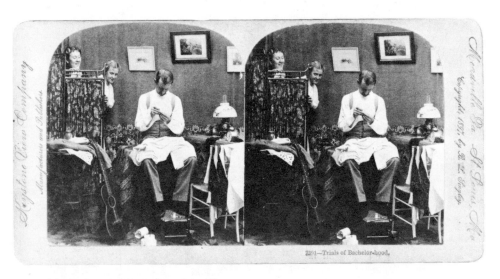

Trials of Bachelor-hood

Stolen Sweets.

There is no Rose without a Thorn.

Every Kiss Has Its Sting.

19

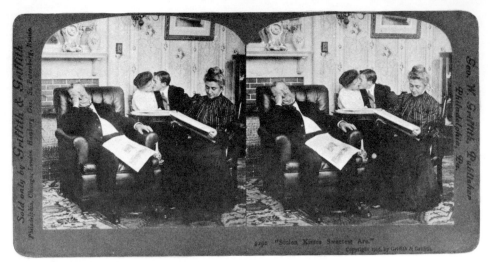

"Stolen Kisses Sweetest Are."

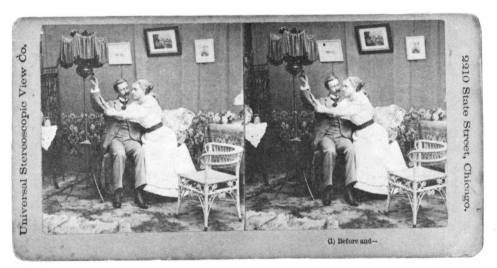

Before and—

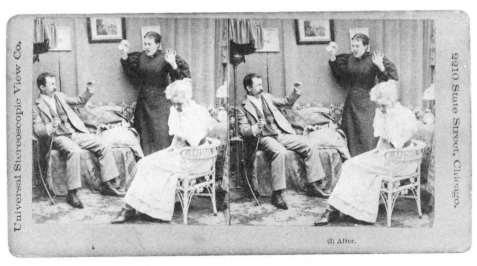

After.

He: "Darling, Let Us Sing, 'I Will Love Thee Ever.'"

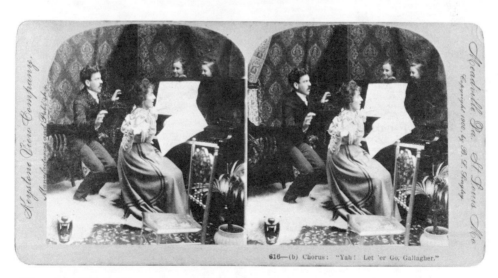

Chorus: "Yah! Let 'er Go, Gallagher."

Won't you come and sit on my lap?

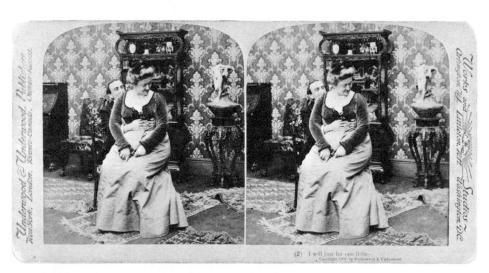

I will just for one little—

Moment!!!

"No, you don't!"

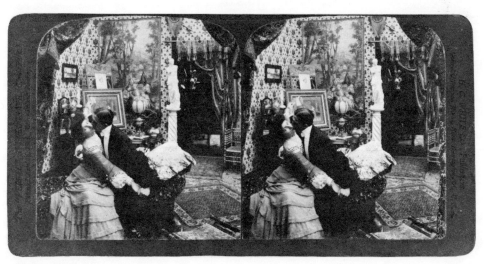

"Yes, I do."

Bliss.

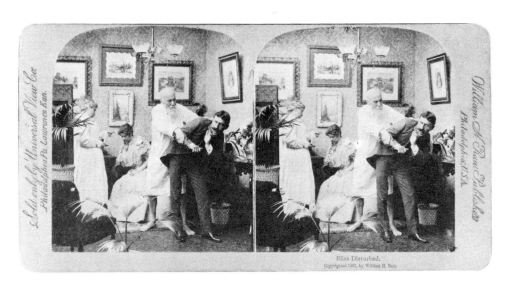

Bliss Disturbed.

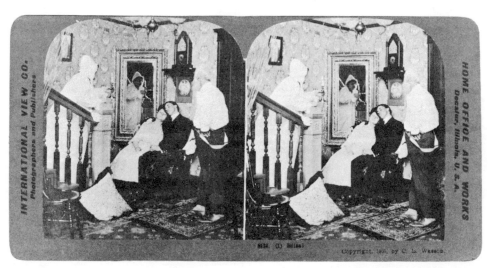

Bliss!

Bliss Disturbed!

Always Take a Horse You Can Drive with One Hand.

A Story without Words.

CONNUBIAL BLISS(TERS)

ADMIRATION—Pierced by Cupid's Dart.

EXPECTATION—Married Life as he pictured it (Music without words).

ELATION—"I've caught Sister this time!"

CONSTERNATION—"Don't you dare tell Father!"

DECLARATION—"Two hearts that beat as one"—but what will Papa say?

ALIENATION—His Wedding Eve at the Bachelor Club.

OBLITERATION—The Wedding Eve bonfire and farewell to former affections.

SOLEMNIZATION—The Nuptial Ceremony.

CONGRATULATION—The Wedding Supper.

ADORATION—Alone at last.

ANTICIPATION—Visions of the future.

INVITATION—"Have wan of your Wife's biscuit!"

VEXATION—"You heartless wretch to call them brick-bats!"

TRIBULATION—Trials of housekeeping, the Cook indisposed.

PRESENTATION—The First Born.

EXASPERATION—Home from the Married Men's Club he fears the Storm.

REALIZATION—Married Life as he found it (Words without Music).

SUBJUGATION—There's no place like home!

Admiring the Wedding Presents—Beware of a Joke.

A Box of Mice among the Wedding Presents.

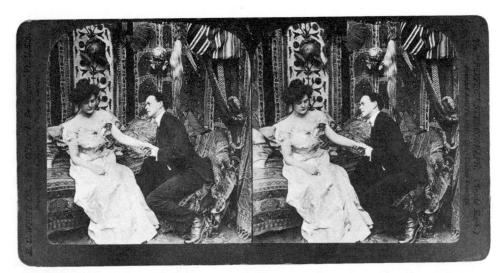

The Proposal.

Dressing the Bride.

The Wedding March.

The Bride.

"With this Ring, I thee Wed."

The Blessing.

Congratulations.

The Wedding Breakfast.

"To the health of the Bride."

"Alone at Last."

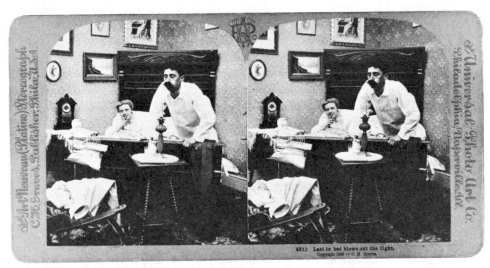

Last in bed blows out the light.

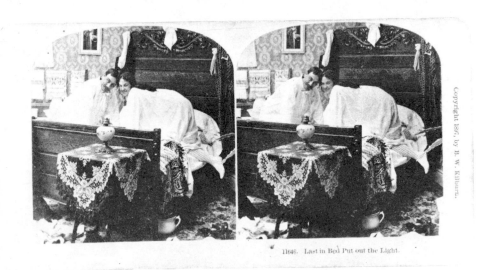

Last in Bed Put out the Light.

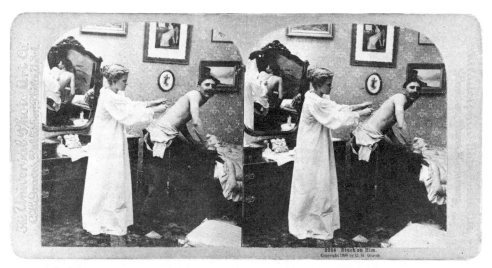

Stuck on Him.

This parting gives me pain, dear.

Before Marriage.

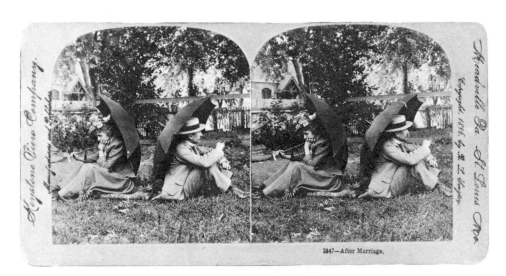

After Marriage.

11:30 P.M. George and Angelina are very fond of sitting up late.

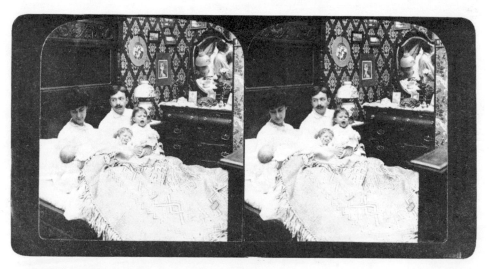

(5 years later) 1:30 A.M. They still sit up late but somehow it is not so much fun as it used to be.

The Floor-walker—by day.

The Floor-walker—by night.

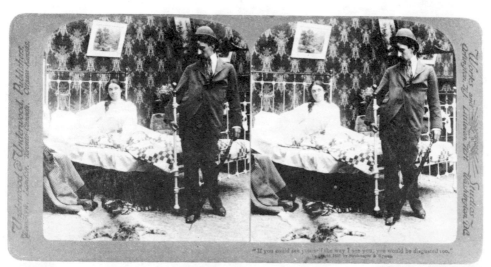

"*If you could see yourself the way I see you, you would be disgusted too.*"

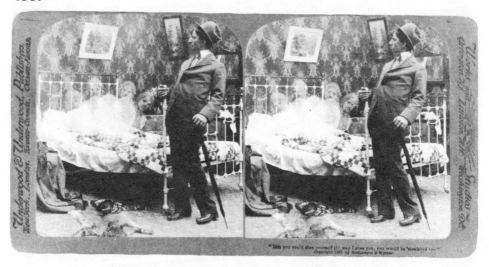

"*I'sh you could shee yourself th' way I shee you, you would be 'stonished too.*"

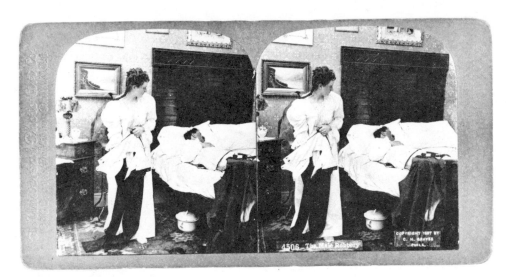

The Male Robbery.

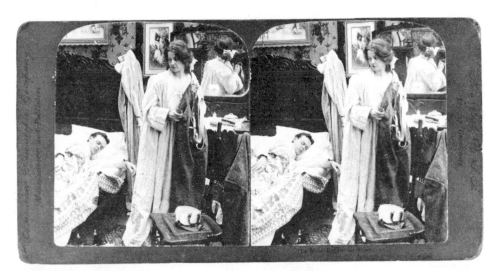

The Male Robber at Work.

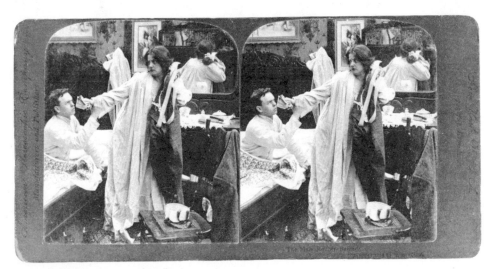

The Male Robber Baffled.

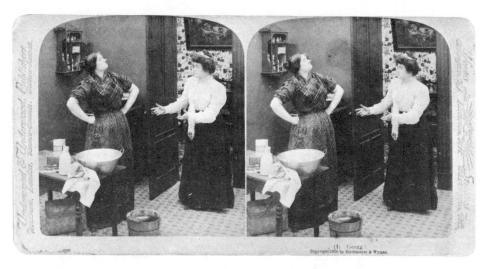

Going!

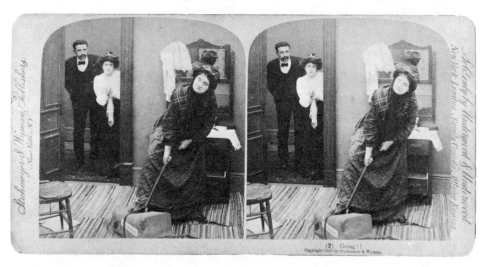

Going!!

Gone!!!

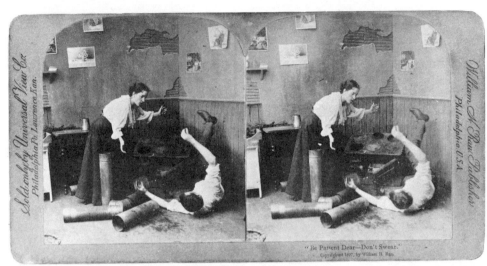

"Be Patient Dear——Don't Swear."

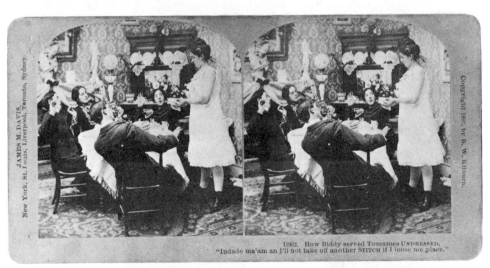

How Biddy served Tomatoes UNDRESSED, "Indade ma'am an I'll not take off another STITCH if I loose me place."

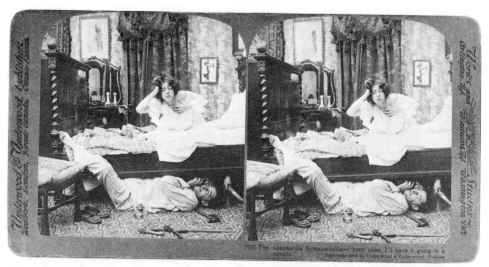

The Automobile Somnambulist—"keep quiet, I'll have it going in a minute."

"For you I left my happy home!"

"You go first, Maria. They wouldn't hurt a woman."

"Sew on your own Buttons. I'm Going for a Ride."

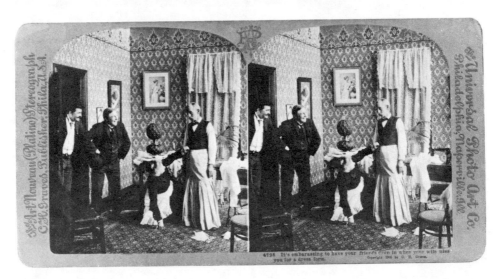

It's embarrassing to have your friends drop in when your wife uses you for a dress form.

"I'll go and get the scissors before I tack this side."

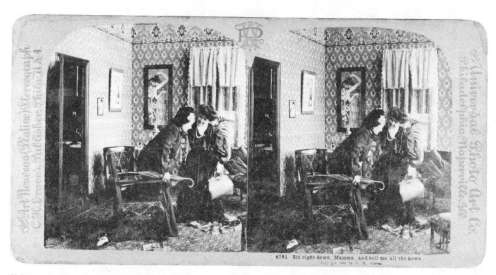

"Sit right down, Mamma, and tell me all the news."

"Help! Help! John! John! Come here, quick!"

"You miserable brute, I'm going home right now!"

"You Wretch! I always told Mary you weren't good enough for her."

Give you a Penny for a Kiss.

She Gets the Kiss.

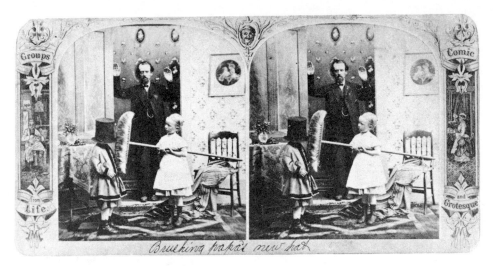

Brushing Papa's new hat.

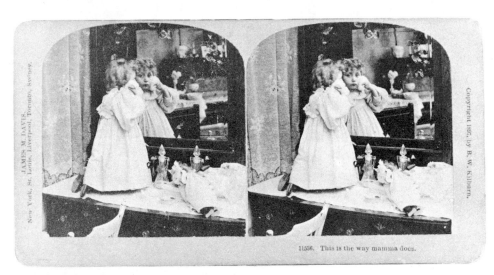

This is the way mamma does.

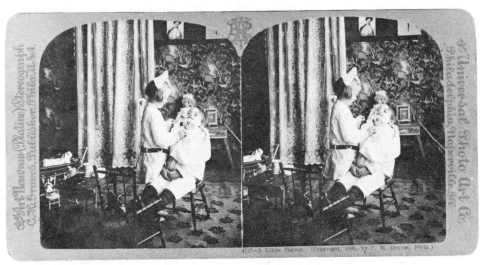

A Little Shaver.

"Of course I'm good—Papa calls me a Holy Terror."

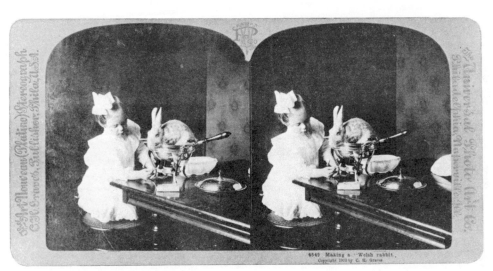

Making a "Welsh rabbit."

Oh, uncle Dave you're just like a real donkey.

In Mischief.

Highway Robbery.

"Come Back! Oh, Come Back!!"

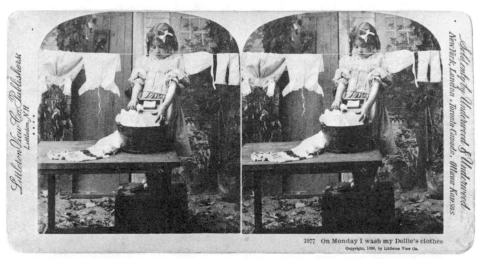

On Monday I wash my Dollie's clothes.

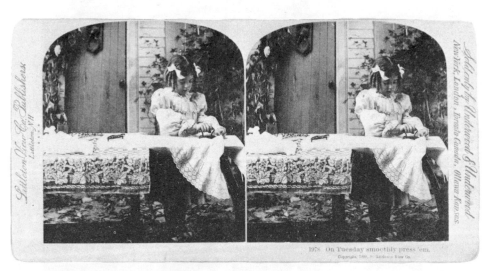

On Tuesday smoothly press 'em.

On Wednesday I mend their little hose.

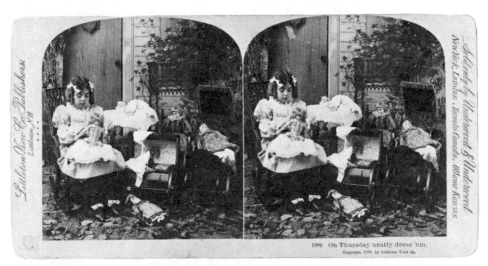

On Thursday neatly dress 'em.

On Friday I play they are taken ill.

On Saturday Cook for Mother.

But when Sunday comes, I say be still, I'm going to Church with Mother.

"I vill practice me dose Intermezzo for der concert tonight."

"Dot music is so lofely it gifs me a thairst like eferyting."

62 *"Now I vill play dot last part ofer again."*

"Dot don't sount like it dit der fairst time."

"I bade you dot I get dot right, so soon as quick."

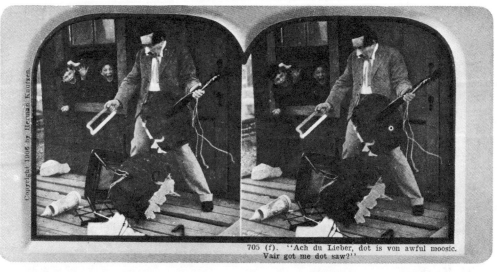

"Ach du Lieber, dot is von awful moosic. Vair got me dot saw?"

63

The start. He vigorously protests.

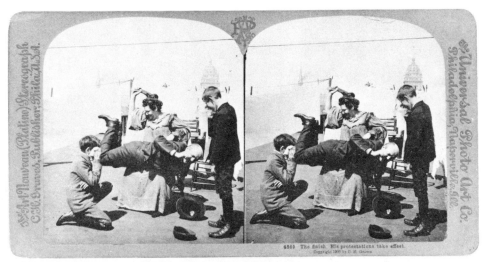

The finish. His protestations take effect.

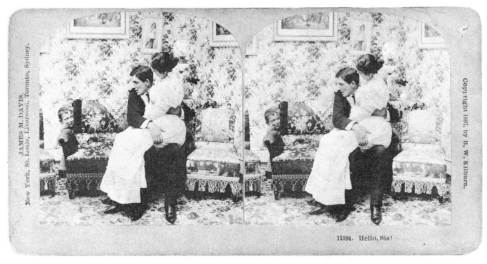

Hello, Sis!

Flirtations

Salutation.

Flirtation.

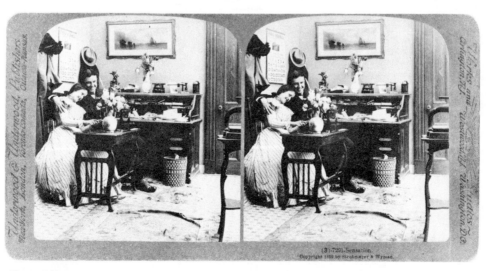

Sensation.

67

Revelation.

Tribulation.

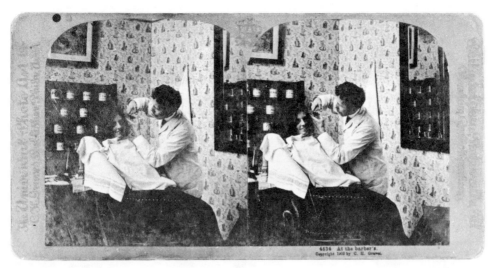

At the barber's.

Getting HER hair banged.

Getting HIS hair banged.

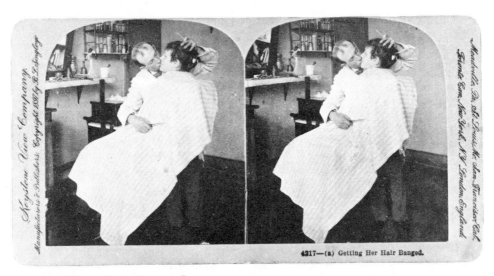

Getting Her Hair Banged.

Getting His Hair Banged.

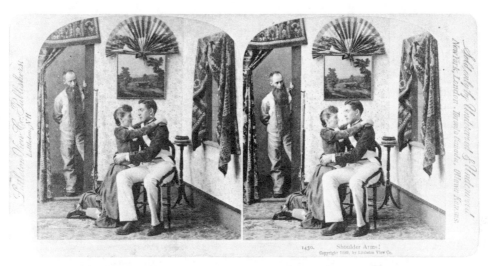

Shoulder Arms!

Charge Bayonets.

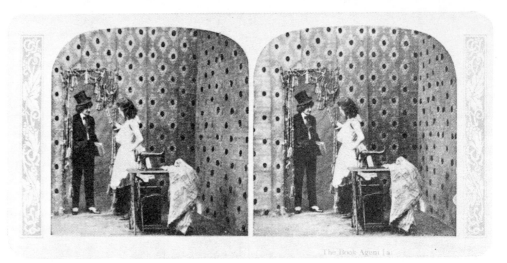

The Book Agent.

The Book Agent. You're a Real Nice Man.

The Book Agent. Spanking the Flirt.

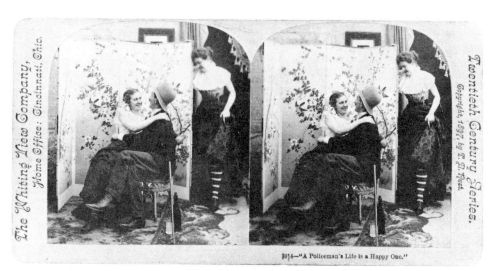

"A Policeman's Life is a Happy One."

The Tipperary Jig.

Sometimes we vote to Mistletoe the World's best fame.

At others—well, the Mistletoe is not to blame!

No, your new type-writer isn't pretty, John, but you'd better try and like her.

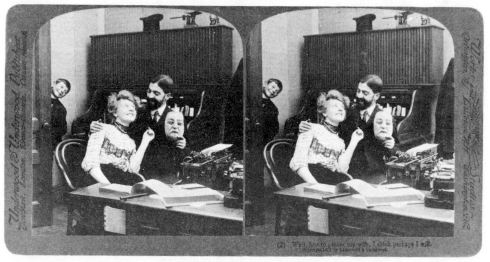

Well, just to please my wife, I think perhaps I will.

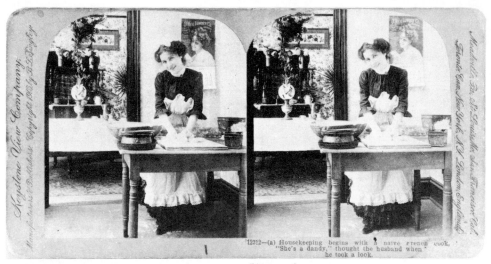

12312—(a) Housekeeping begins with a naive French cook,
"She's a dandy," thought the husband when he took a look.

Housekeeping begins with a naive French cook,
"She's a dandy," thought the husband when he took a look.

12313—(b) "Ah, ha! I see why I'm forbidden the kitchen,
It's because the cook is so bewitchin'."

"Ah, ha! I see why I'm forbidden the kitchen,
It's because the cook is so bewitchin'."

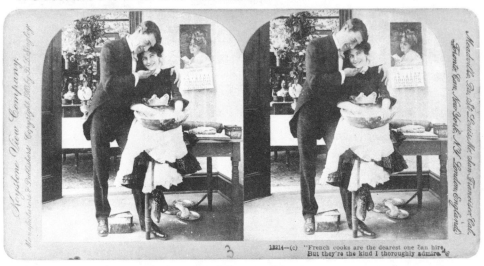

12314—(c) "French cooks are the dearest one can hire,
But they're the kind I thoroughly admire."

"French cooks are the dearest one can hire,
But they're the kind I thoroughly admire."

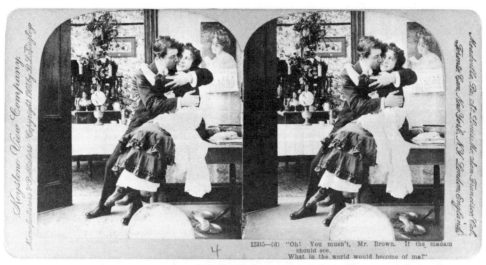

"Oh! You musn't, Mr. Brown. If the madam should see,
What in the world would become of me?"

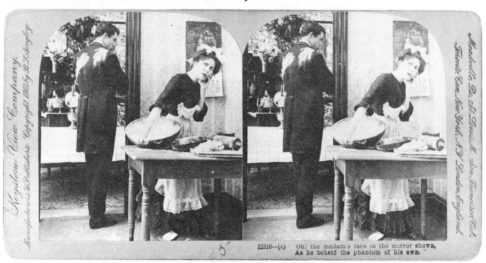

Oh! the madam's face in the mirror shown,
As he beheld the phantom of his own.

"Wait a moment till I see what those hand prints mean!
You have been to the kitchen, it's plain to be seen."

"You brazen huzzy! You shall leave at this hour!
And the least of your fault is the wasted flour."

"Oh, you wretch! this I shall not endure.
I shall fire that flirt and a divorce procure."

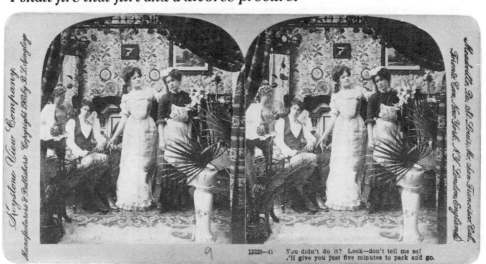

"You didn't do it? Look—don't tell me so!
I'll give you just five minutes to pack and go."

"Au Revoir! Mr. Brown, a helping hand I know you'll lend,
If I should need a recommend."

"O, you're so sweet! And those beautiful eyes!
By that tricky cook I was hypnotized."

The Halloween Party—Ducking for apples.

The Halloween Party—"Can't I get in the game?"

The Halloween Party—"Oh, yes, if you insist."

Hallow e'en Party. An Intruder.

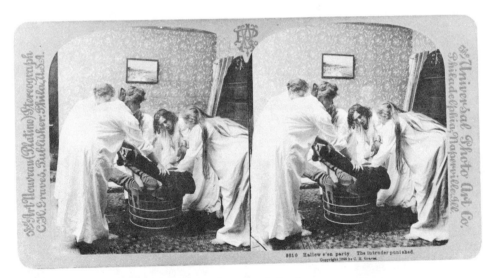

Hallow e'en party. The intruder punished.

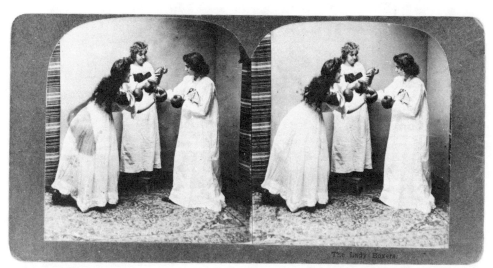

The Lady Boxers.

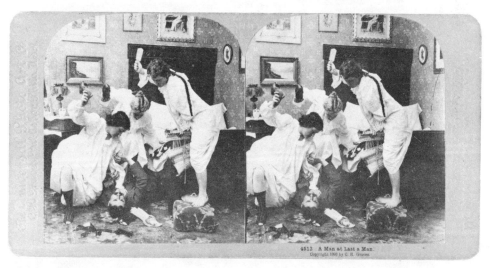

A Man at Last a Man.

Yes, Mr. Caught-a-tarter! the time is coming when—

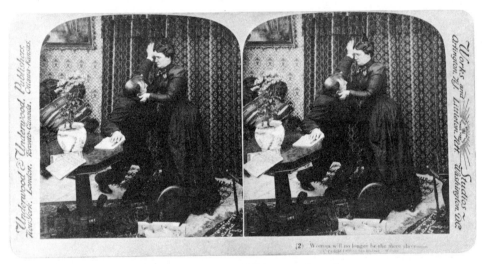

Woman will no longer be the mere slave—

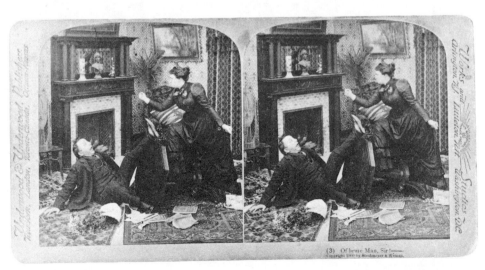

Of brute Man, Sir!—

No longer be the poor down-trodden—

Oppressed—

Weak and helpless being she now is!

He stoops to serve.

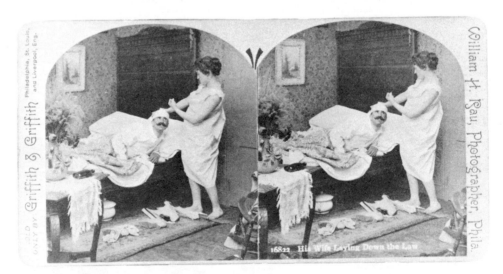

His Wife Laying Down the Law.

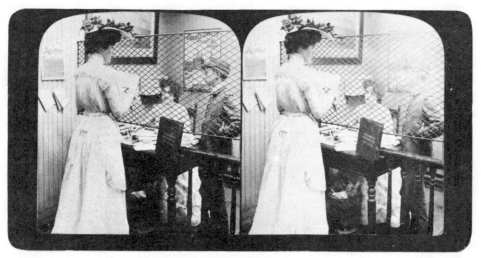

Quick *way to spread news,*—telegraph.

Quicker *way to spread news,*—telephone.

Quickest *way to spread news,*—tell a woman!

A Shady Nook, A Rippling Brook and not a Man in Sight.

Trying the High Kick.

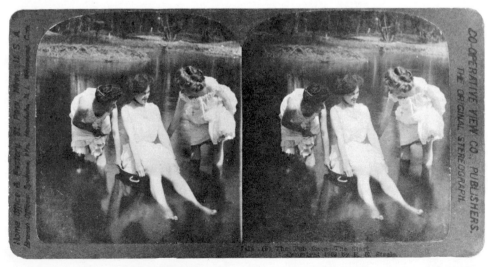

The Tub Race—The Start.

An Interruption—"O Horrors! a Man and a Camera, too."

"How Dare You take our Picture—Throw Him into the River, Girls."

A Doubtful Triumph—Collapse after the Struggle.

Facing the Adversary.

Thrust and Parry.

Revenged.

Reconciliation.

The Vanquished.

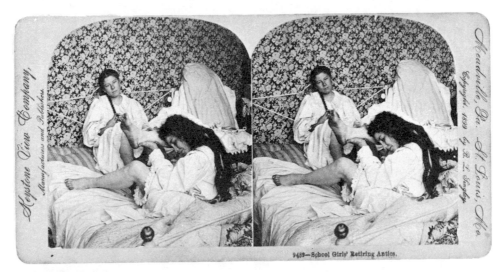

School Girls' Retiring Antics.

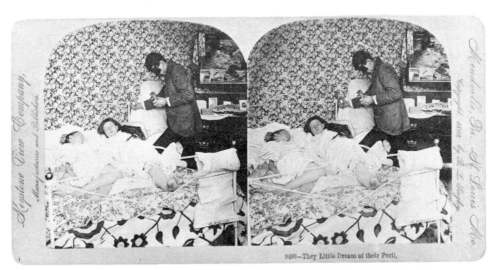

They Little Dream of their Peril.

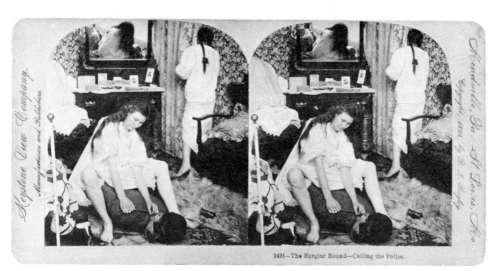

The Burglar Bound—Calling the Police.

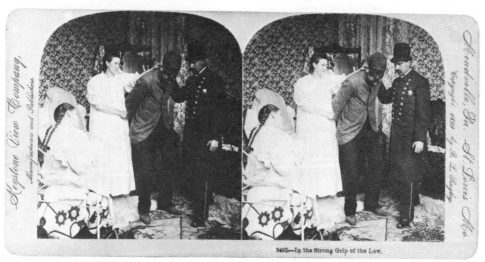

In the Strong Grip of the Law.

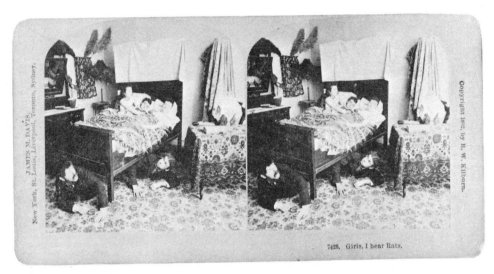

Girls, I hear Rats.

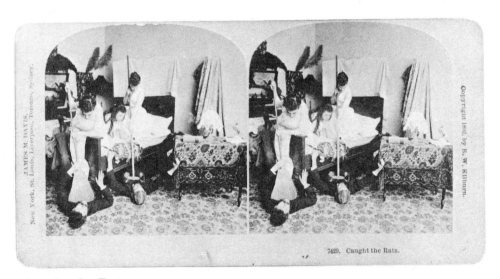

Caught the Rats.

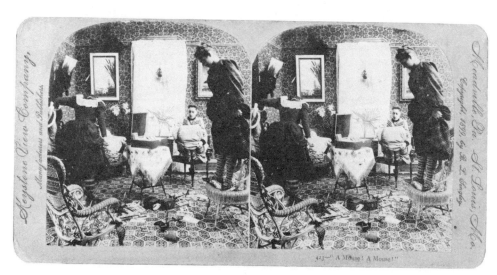

"A Mouse! A Mouse!"

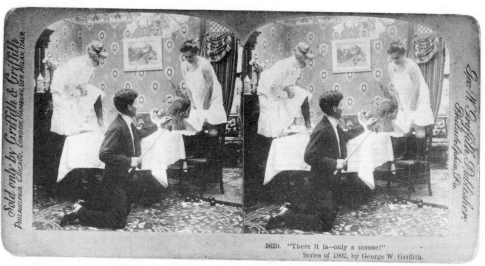

"There it is—only a mouse!"

The Conquered Garter.

A sad predicament—He wants to go home.

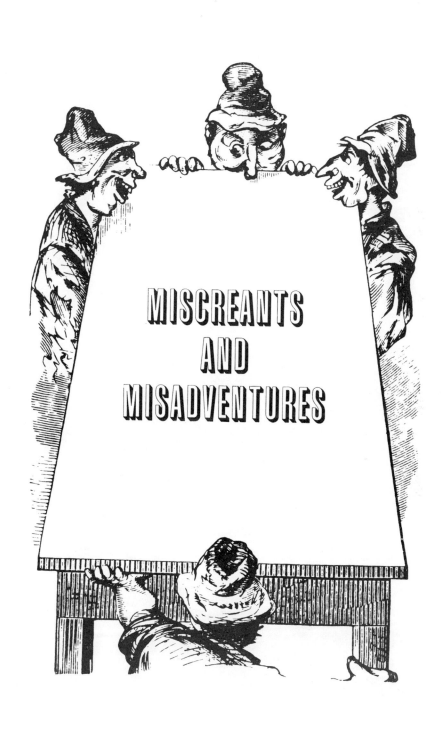

MISCREANTS
AND
MISADVENTURES

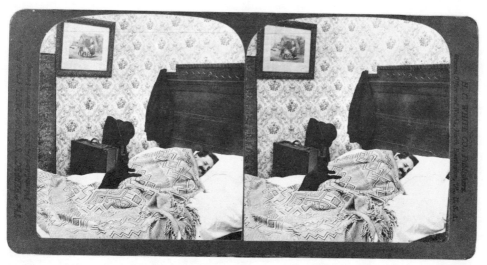

"Don't shoot! My pocket book is under the pillow."

"Stealing My Eggs, Are You?"

"Pa, Don't You Know Your Own Daughter?"

The Midnight Spread.—"Girls! what if Miss Grey should come."

Injured Innocence.—"Really, Miss Grey, it must have been some other room."

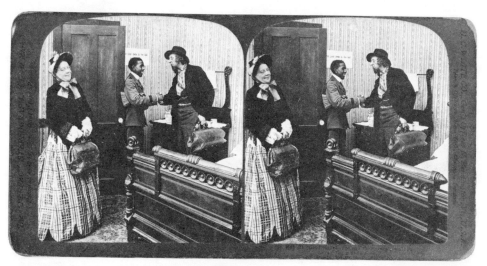

"Good night! See ye i' the mornin'; wu'll be daown 'baout nye a'clock."

"By durn, Samenthy, this beats the old pump all holler. Push jest a leetle harder and she'll be here."

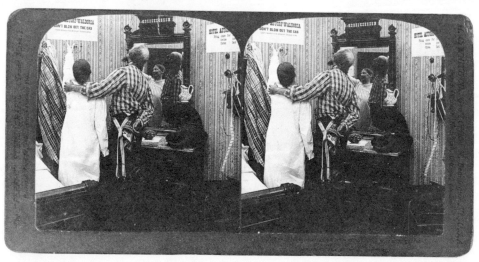

"What on arth do folks want to stay up after midnight for and pay for extry lights?"

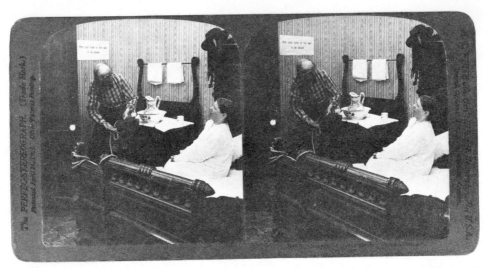

"Naow, Silas, if yeow put them boots aout that way, they'll steal 'em sure!"

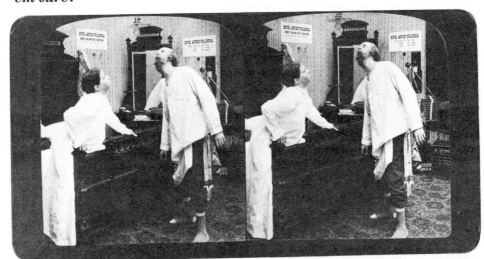

"Gosh all hemlock, we can't blow that air thing aout, lights after midnight charged extry—they're baound to get ye sumhaow."

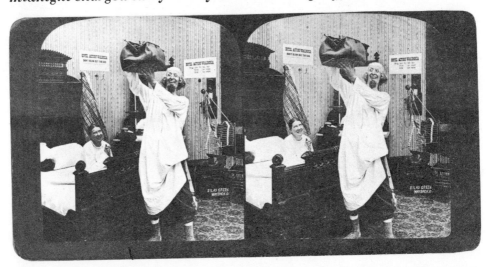

"By gosh, Menthy, this'll fix it. Naow we can sleep and not pay for extry lights."

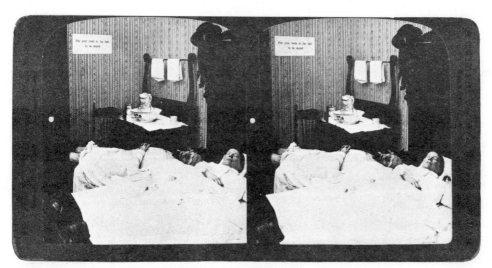

Silas puts his boots in the hall to be shined but decides to take no chances of losing them.

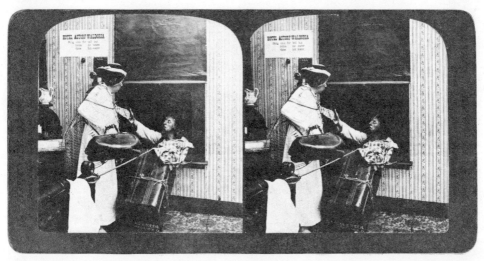

In the early morning, a false alarm of fire hastens their departure and they leave on the first train for Wayback.

A train robber holding up a train.

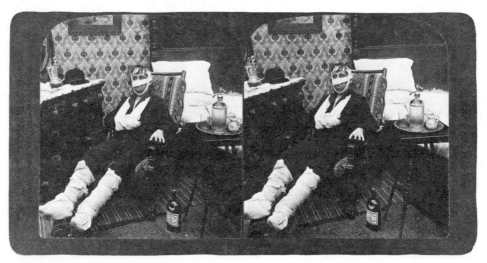

"A case of Ale." (Ail.)

704 (a). Such a toothache! He would give anything
to have it out.

Such a toothache! He would give anything to have it out.

704 (b). "Just a minute, now. It won't hurt you."

"Just a minute, now. It won't hurt you."

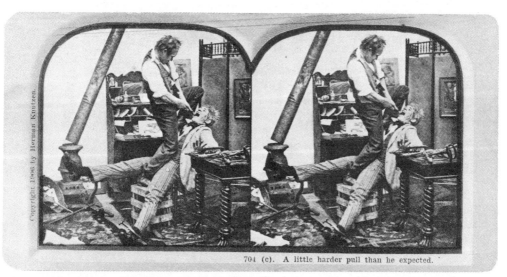

704 (c). A little harder pull than he expected.

A little harder pull than he expected.

704 (d). "With the ice tongs. Pull it or bust something.

With the ice tongs. Pull it or bust something.

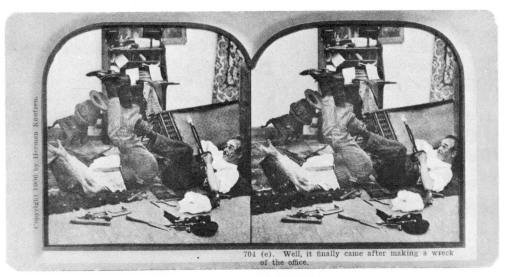

704 (e). Well, it finally came after making a wreck of the office.

Well, it finally came after making a wreck of the office.

704 (f). Now the tooth is out let the dentist whistle for his pay.

Now the tooth is out let the dentist whistle for his pay.

Dear father: Send me $27 quick for Gibbon's Rome in nine volumes.

————! ————! ————! He sent me the books.

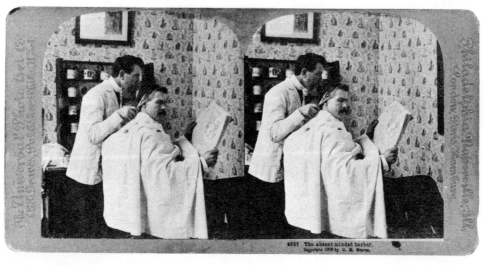

The absent minded barber.